The synagogue is a special place. Sometimes we call the synagogue
Bet Tefillah—a House of Prayer. Jewish people come to the synagogue to pray.
Sometimes we call the synagogue *Bet Midrash*, a House of Study, because
Jews also come here to study. Every synagogue has its own name. What is the
name of your synagogue? Can you find out what the name of your synagogue
means? Finish the picture. Try to make this building look like your own
synagogue. Then write the name of your synagogue above the doors.

Mezuzah means "doorpost." It is a small case made of wood or metal. It is hung on the doorpost of a Jewish home or building. Inside the *Mezuzah* is a small roll of special paper called parchment. On the parchment is written the *Sh'ma*, a very important prayer. The *Sh'ma* reminds us that there is only one God. Inside the *Mezuzah* are other prayers from the Bible, too. Color in the letters of the *Sh'ma* and learn to say the prayer by heart. Then cut it out and put it inside the *Mezuzah* case on the next page.

Here is a *Mezuzah* case that you can make. The Hebrew letter *shin* on the case stands for *Shaddai* which means God. First color the *Mezuzah* and then cut it out carefully. Fold on the lines. Roll up the *Sh'ma* prayer and put it inside the case before you paste it together. You can hang this *Mezuzah* on the doorpost of your own bedroom at home.

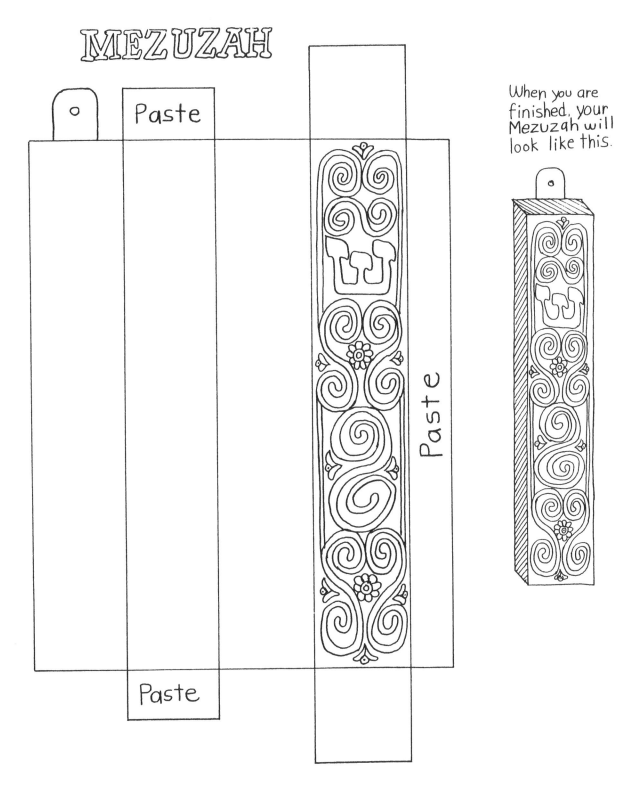

MEZUZAH

Paste

Paste

Paste

Paste

When you are finished, your Mezuzah will look like this.

The *Aron Ha Kodesh* is the Holy Ark. It is the holiest place in the synagogue. The ark is set on the *Bimah*, a raised platform, against a wall that faces the East. We face the ark when we pray. Then we are facing in the direction of Jerusalem. We keep something very important in the *Aron Ha Kodesh*. Connect the dots to see what is inside the Holy Ark.

A *Ner Tamid* is an Eternal Light. The Eternal Light always hangs above the *Aron Ha Kodesh.* Eternal means forever. This special light is never turned off. It stays on all the time as a reminder that God is forever. Placing a light over the Holy Ark also reminds us that the Torah inside the Ark brightens our way. Color the letters on the Eternal Light. They spell the words *Ner Tamid* in Hebrew. Color the flame, too. Then your *Ner Tamid* will be lit like the one over the Holy Ark in your synagogue.

A special curtain hangs just inside the doors of the Holy Ark. It is called a *Parochet.* This curtain is made of velvet, silk or satin. It is often covered with a design. The two lions remind us of a saying: "You should be as strong as a lion to do the will of God." Color the design on this *Parochet.* Make it as beautiful as you can.

There are five books in the Torah. They are called The Five Books of Moses. The Torah tells us the story of the Jewish people and how they lived long ago. The Torah tells us about God. The Torah is also called the Law. It teaches us our laws and explains how we can be good people. Learn the names of The Five Books of Moses. Color each book with a different color crayon. Then use all five crayons to color the Torah.

A *Sofer* is a specially trained scribe who is very religious. He writes each word of the Torah with a feather pen and a special kind of ink. The Torah is written on parchment, the skin of an animal. Parchment lasts for a very long time. Pretend that you are a *Sofer* and that your black crayon or marker is a feather pen. Carefully color each Hebrew letter. Every letter in the Torah must be perfect.

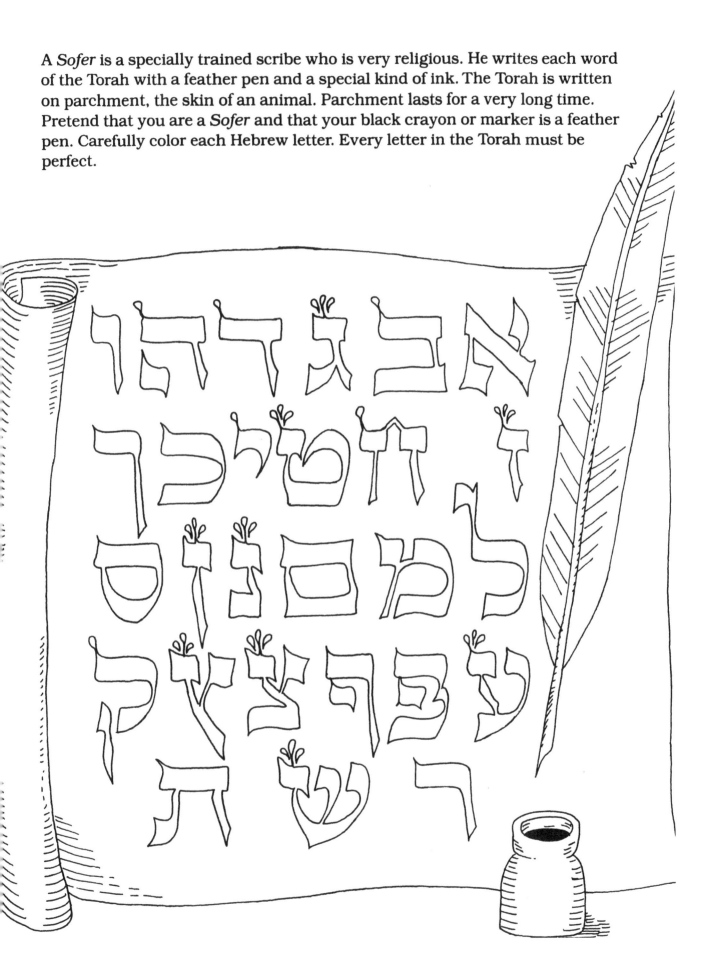

The Torah scroll is on wooden rollers. The beginning and the end of the Torah are each attached to a roller. Each roller is called *Aytz Hayim*. The Hebrew words *Aytz Hayim* help us to remember what the Torah is. Connect the dotted letters on the wooden rollers to see what the Hebrew words mean.

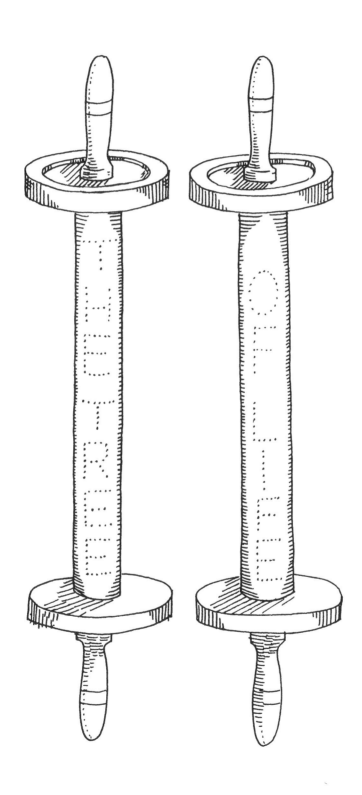

This Torah is rolled open to the very beginning. The first Hebrew word in the Torah means "in the beginning." In Hebrew it is pronounced *B'ray-sheet.* This is also the Hebrew for *Genesis*, the name of the first book of the Torah. This book tells the story of how the world was created. Color the Hebrew letters with a black crayon or marker to make the Hebrew word stand out.

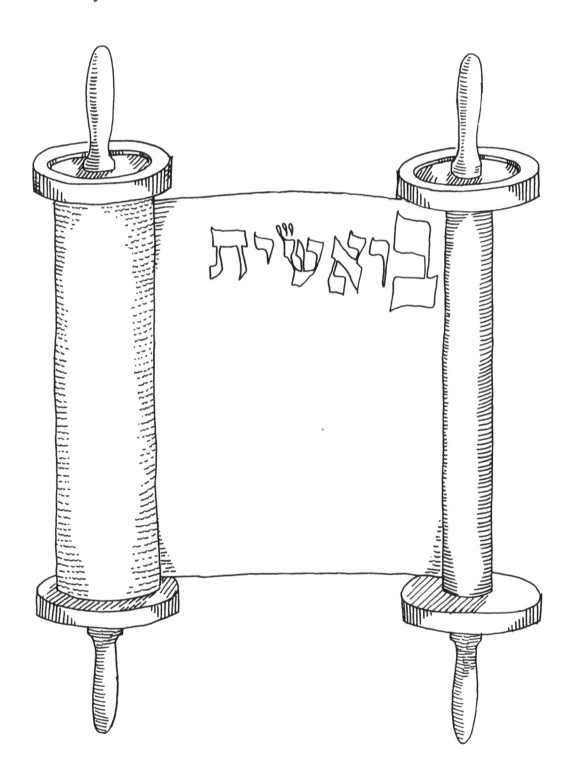

This Torah is rolled open to the very end. The last word in the Torah is *Yisrael*. It means "Israel." *Yisrael* is the name of the Jewish people. It is also the name of our Land. Color the Hebrew letters with a black crayon or marker to make the Hebrew word stand out.

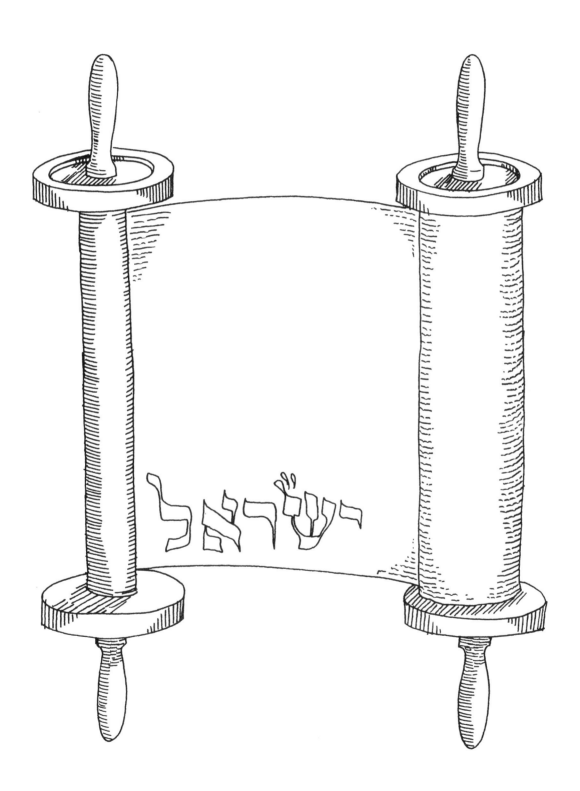

When something is important, we find ways to protect it. The Torah is very important. We want to protect the Torah. That is why we have a Torah binder, or *Cha-Go-Rah*. The Torah binder is made of strong and beautiful material. It is a narrow strip of heavy cloth with metal buckles at each end. The Torah binder keeps the Torah rolled up tightly. Trace your way from the beginning of the Torah binder to the end. Then color the *Cha-Go-Rah* so that it is nice enough to place around a Torah.

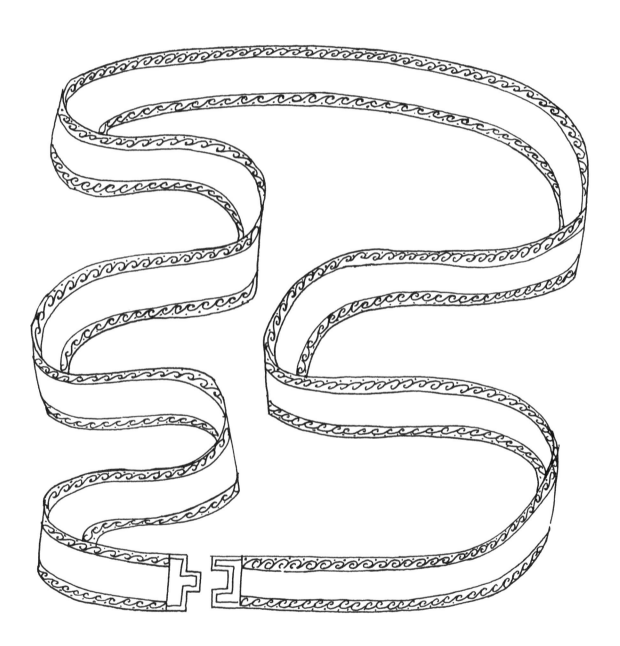

The Torah is dressed in a special covering when it is in the Holy Ark. The Torah is covered with a mantle or *K'Tonet.* It is covered to protect it and to make it beautiful. During the year, the mantle may be any color. During the High Holy Days, the *K'Tonet* is white. Color the design on the *K'Tonet.*

A silver Breastplate is used to decorate the Torah. The chain of the Breastplate hangs over the *Aytz Chayim* rollers. The silver is engraved with a design. In Hebrew the Breastplate is called either a *Tzitz* or a *Hoshen.* This Breastplate contains the first ten letters of the Hebrew alphabet. Do you know what these letters stand for? Connect the dots to engrave a design on this silver Breastplate.

To finish dressing the Torah, we put a wonderful crown on top. We dress the Torah like a king. The crown is made of silver. It often has bells on it. The Torah crown is called a *Keter*. Color the crown. Find the Hebrew letters that spell the Hebrew word *Keter*. Then color in the letters.

A *Yad* is a silver pointer. We use it to point to each word when we read from the Torah. We also use the pointer so that we will not touch the Torah with our fingers. *Yad* is the Hebrew word for "hand." First find the arrow. Then color your way from the end of the *Yad* to the Hebrew words in the Torah. Do you know what these Hebrew words are?

שְׁמַע יִשְׂרָאֵל

Here is everything you need to dress the Torah. Carefully color and cut out each piece. Then paste the pieces on the Torah on the next page.

It is an honor to hold up and to dress the Torah in the synagogue. Two people are chosen. They are called *Hagbahah* and *Gelilah*. *Hagbahah* lifts up the Torah for all to see. *Gelilah* rolls the Torah tightly and then places the binder, mantle, breastplate, yad and crown on the Torah. Dress the Torah below.

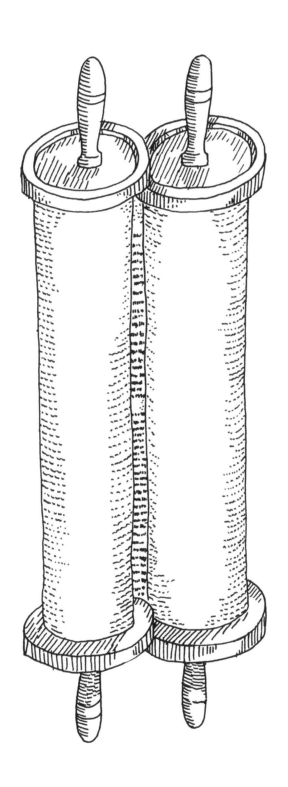

After the Torah is read, it is carried around the synagogue. All the people have a chance to be close to the Torah. The Torah parade is called a *Hakkafah*. Take the Torah on a *Hakkafah* all around the synagogue. Then return it to the *Aron Ha Kodesh*.

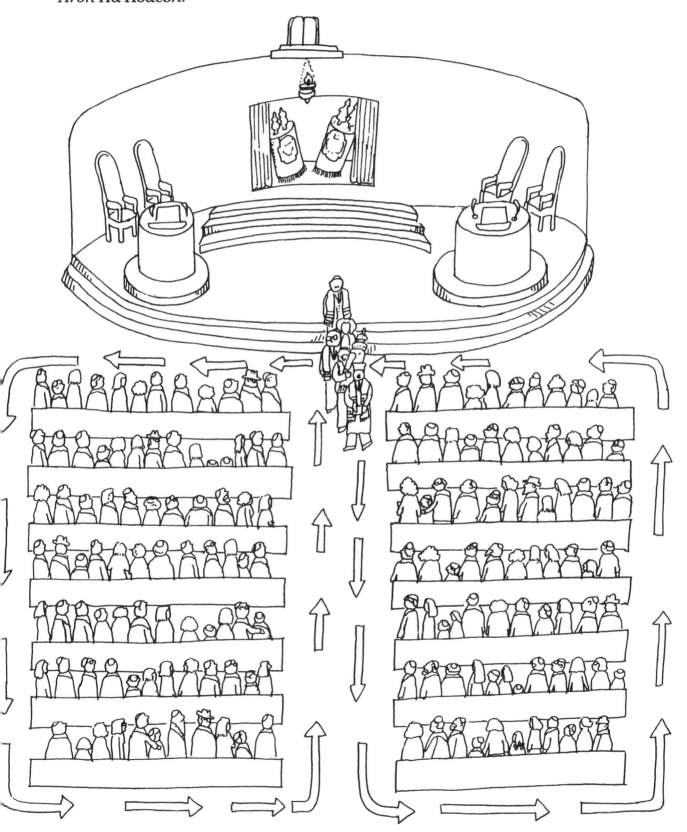

The Hebrew word Rabbi means "my teacher." The Rabbi teaches us about the Jewish religion. The Rabbi leads parts of the synagogue service. The Rabbi helps people to celebrate their happy times and also when they are sad. What is your Rabbi's name? Can you make this picture look like your Rabbi?

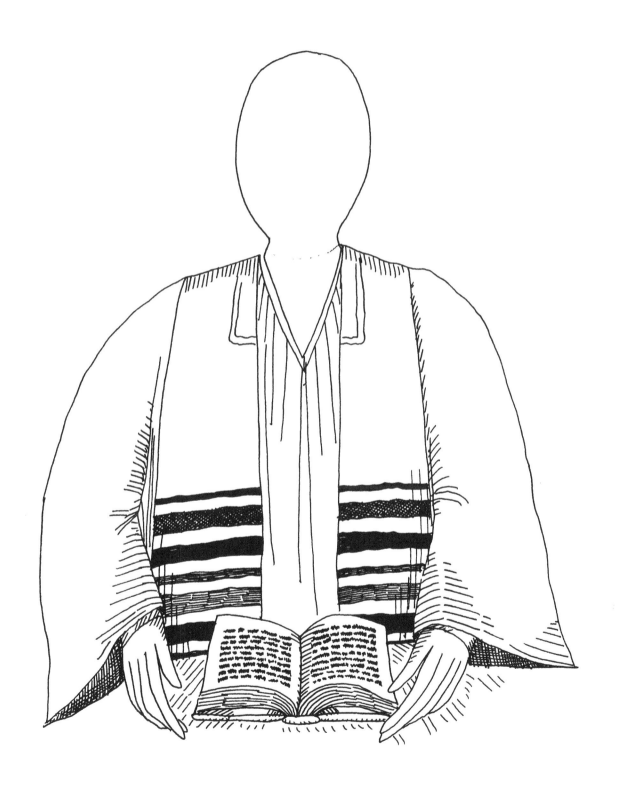

Many synagogues have a Cantor. The Cantor has a beautiful singing voice. The Cantor leads us in song during the synagogue service. Sometimes the Cantor teaches music in the religious school and often prepares students for Bar and Bat Mitzvah. In Hebrew Cantor is *Hazan.* What is your Cantor's name? Can you make this picture look like your *Hazan*?

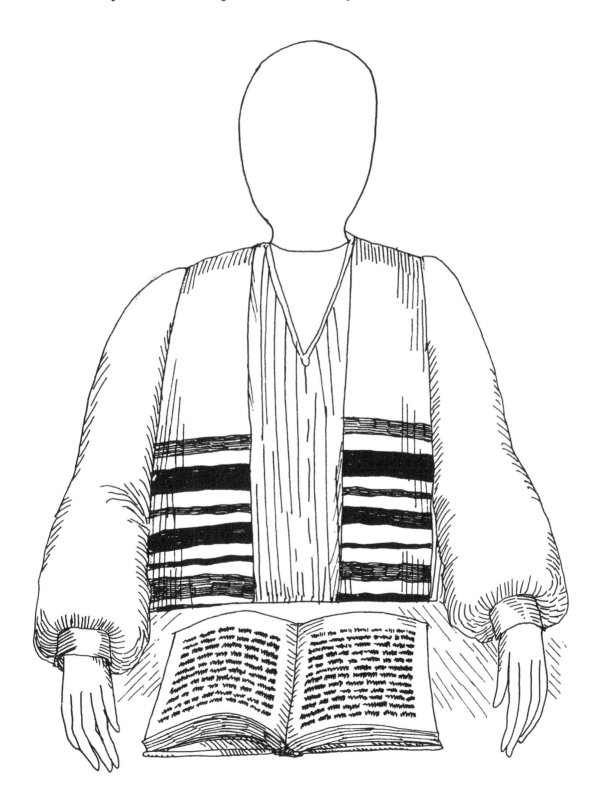

A *Siddur* is a prayerbook. It is used for praying on weekdays, on Shabbat, and on Festivals. The *Siddur* contains many prayers, poems and songs. They are in a special order. The Hebrew word *Siddur* comes from the Hebrew word *seder* which means "order." Design a special cover for this *Siddur*.

Many people cover their heads when they pray. They wear a *Kipah* to show their respect to God. Sometimes the *Kipah* is embroidered with colorful silk thread. Connect the dots on the *Kipah* with colored pencils or markers. When you are finished, the picture will look like an embroidered *Kipah*.

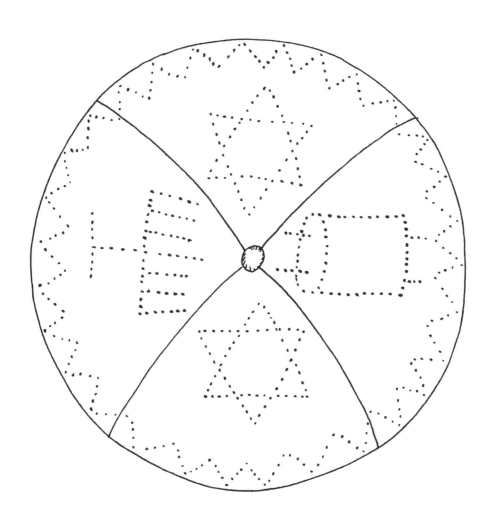

Many people wear a *Tallit* when they pray. The *Tallit* is worn during morning services in the synagogue. It reminds us to keep God's commandments. The *Tallit* is a long piece of cloth. On each end of the *Tallit* there are fringes which are knotted together in a special way. Let the person in this *Tallit* be you. Try to show how you feel when you pray.

On weekdays, some people wear *Tefillin* when they pray. *Tefillin* are small leather boxes with little scrolls of parchment inside. Words from the Bible are written on the scrolls. One part of the *Tefillin* is worn on the forehead. The other part is worn on the left arm and hand. Use a black crayon or marker to color in the straps of the *Tefillin*. You will see how it looks on a person's head and the design it makes on a person's arm.

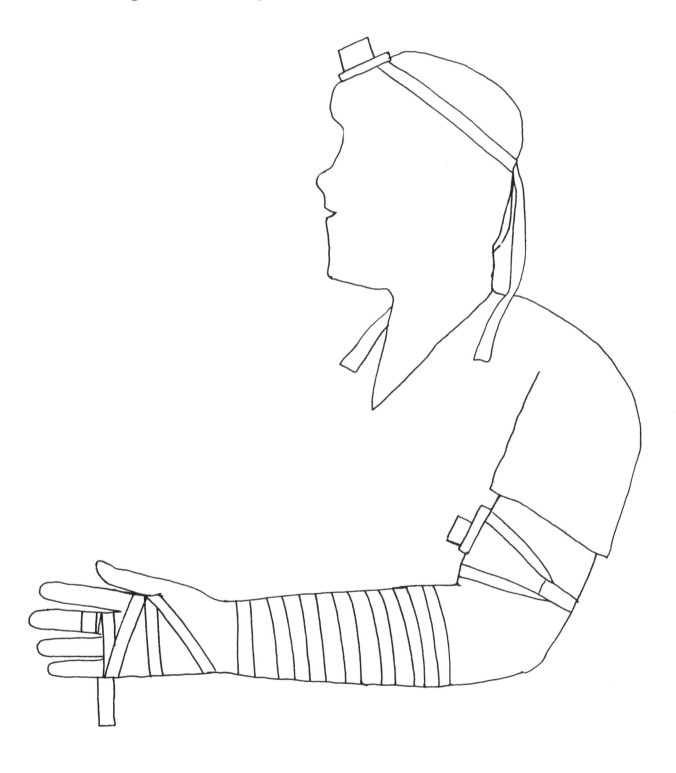

You know the three things that some Jewish people wear when they pray. Cut out the *Tallit, Kipah* and *Tefillin*. Then paste them on the picture of the boy so he will be ready to pray.

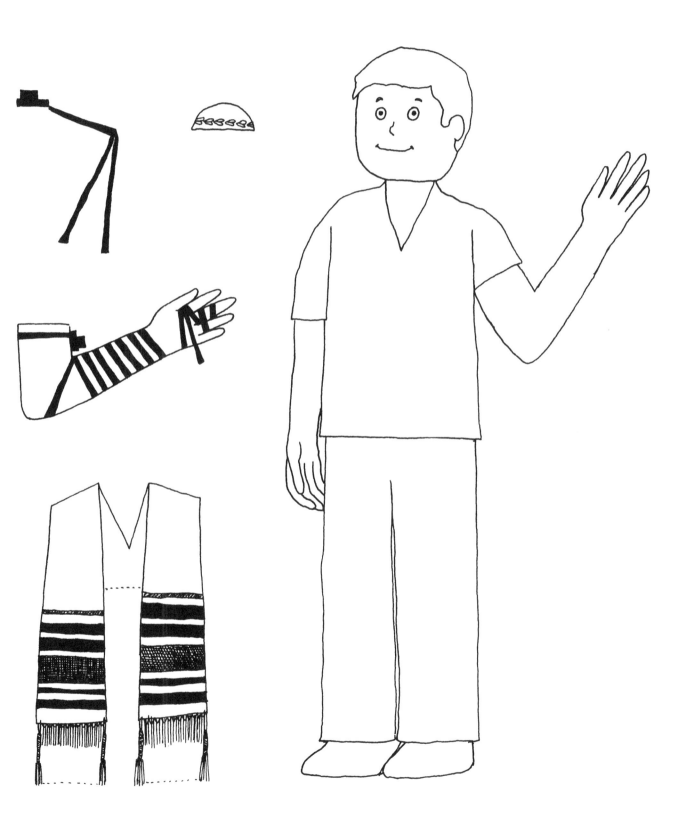

The Ten Commandments are very important laws. They help us to live good lives. The Ten Commandments were carved on tablets made of stone. The stone tablets are called *Luchot* in Hebrew. Each of the Hebrew letters on the *Luchot* stands for a number. Color each Hebrew letter carefully to see the shapes more clearly. Then learn the name and the number of each Hebrew letter.

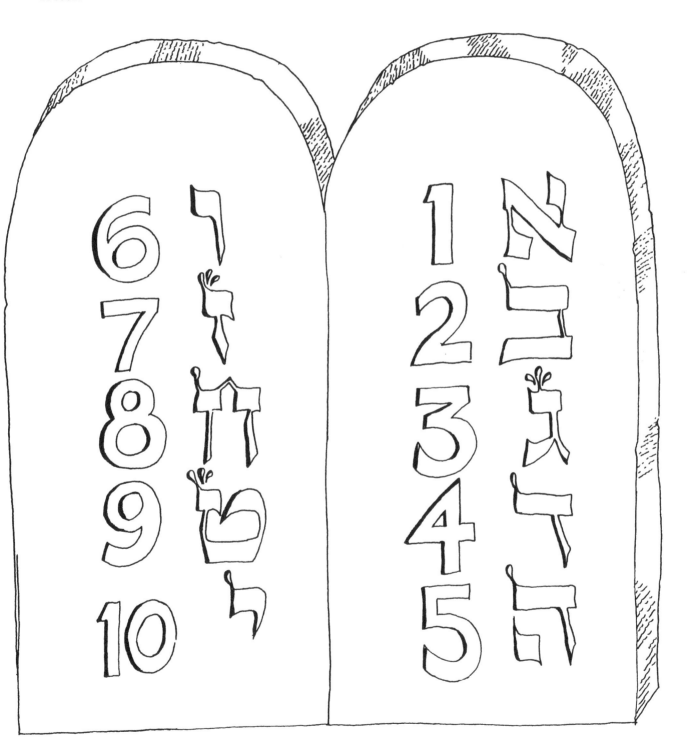

Many synagogues have large candlesticks called a *Menorah*. Sometimes the *Menorah* is very tall, even taller than a person. A *Menorah* was used many, many years ago in our ancient Temple to give light. The *Menorah* reminds us that our religion has lived for thousands of years. Light the candles by coloring in the flames. Then count them to see how many candles there are in a *Menorah*.

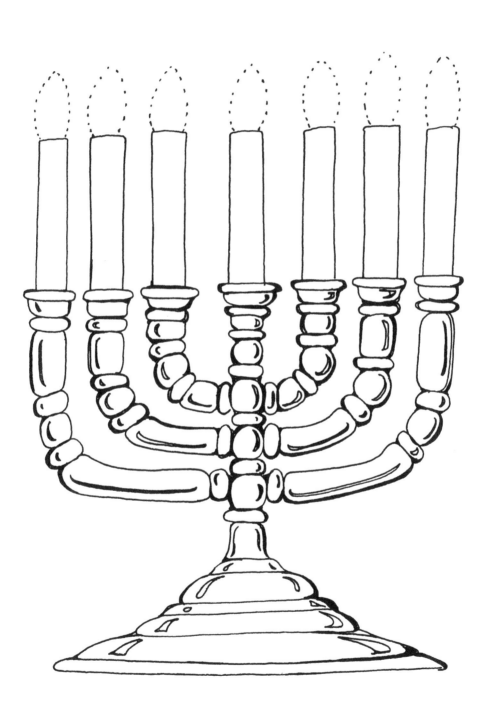

Many synagogues have windows made of colored glass. They are called stained glass windows. They help make the synagogue look beautiful. Color in the stained glass window with different crayons. When you are finished, you can hang your picture on the window of your classroom or on your window at home.

The *Magen David* is a six pointed star. Some people call it a Jewish star. The Hebrew words *Magen David* mean "Shield of David." The *Magen David* is the symbol of Jewish people everywhere. It is on the flag of the State of Israel. Show that you are part of the Jewish People by writing your name inside the *Magen David*. Can you write your name in Hebrew? Use the second line. Color the points of the star with your blue crayon.

MAGEN DAVID מָגֵן דָּוִד

Each card has a picture of a Jewish symbol on it. Cut out the cards.
Match each picture card with its name on the next page. Or you can play
a GO FISH GAME with a friend. Put two sets of picture cards together.
When you have a match, you keep the cards and take another turn.
The player with the most cards is the winner.

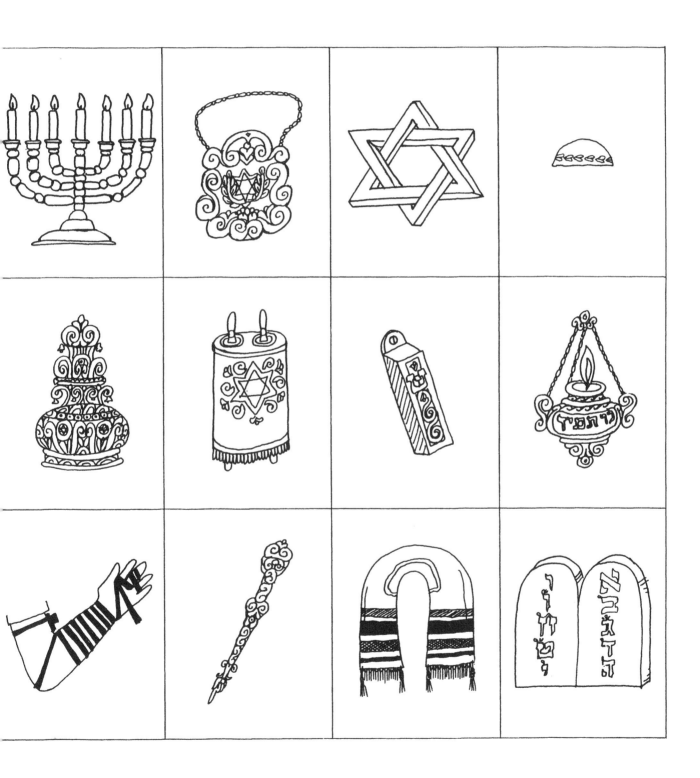

Each card has the name of a Jewish symbol on it. Cut out the cards.
Match each name with its picture. Or you can play a CONCENTRATION GAME.
Place the picture and word cards face down. Pick one at a time.
When you match a symbol to its name, you keep the cards and take another turn.
The player with the most cards is the winner.

MEZUZAH	**NER TAMID**	**K'TONET**	**KETER**
TZITZ or HOSHEN	**YAD**	**MAGEN DAVID**	**KIPAH**
MENORAH	**LUCHOT**	**TEFILLIN**	**TALLIT**

www.ingramcontent.com/pod-product-compliance
Lightning Source LLC
Jackson TN
JSHW061855030225
78354JS00005B/35